UNDER

THE

VULTURE-TREE

Books by David Bottoms

POETRY

Under the Vulture-Tree
In a U-Haul North of Damascus
Shooting Rats at the Bibb County Dump
Jamming With the Band at the VFW (limited edition)

FICTION

Any Cold Jordan

ANTHOLOGIES

The Morrow Anthology of Younger American Poets (editor)

UNDER THE VULTURE-TREE

David Bottoms

QUILL WILLIAM MORROW
New York

Grateful acknowledgment is made to the editors of the following magazines in the pages of which the contents of this book first appeared: *American Poetry Review, Atlantic Monthly, The Bennington Review, The Kenyon Review, The Missouri Review, New Virginia Review, The New Yorker, The North American Review, Oxford Poetry, Poetry, The Southern Review,* and *The Virginia Quarterly Review.*

The author would like to thank the editors of *Poetry* magazine for their kind support in awarding him their Levinson Prize.

Library of Congress Cataloging-in-Publication Data

Bottoms, David.
Under the vulture-tree.

I. Title.
PS3552.0819U5 1987 811'.54 86-33178
ISBN 0-688-06834-0
ISBN 0-688-07148-1 (pbk.)

Printed in the United States of America

First Quill Edition

1 2 3 4 5 6 7 8 9 10

BOOK DESIGN BY DALE COTTON

for Maria Guarnaschelli and Maria Carvainis

CONTENTS

I

In the Ice Pasture

Something cried in the field and I took the binoculars
into the yard, the zeroing wind,
saw in what starlight the glasses gathered
the gray barn, the empty pasture haunted
with trees, nothing.
And then in patches the deep prints
tracking the hill, the snow trail floating
over the broken fence
where the horse walked fifty yards onto the pond
to fall neck-deep through the ice.

What was he trying to become out there,
thrashing to get a hoof up
like an odd beast cracking his shell?

I ran to the basement for an ax
and out the basement door, outrunning my breath
to the edge of the bank,
where he calmed to watch me tap with the handle,
creep three-legged onto the pond,
as though he wanted me to witness the beauty
of his change—only a quiver of the head
as he waited,
half a white statue in a fountain of ice.

Sleet, like static, crackled the pond
as I eased him back from the blade of the ax.
Then behind me a noise like the snapping of bones
and my feet stood on nothing as I grabbed
for his mane, sank chest-deep
in the shock of the cold,

both of us sinking, hooves
pounding legs, kicking me under.

How long did I hang there, numb,
bodiless, before the body of the horse rose under me
and what we were lunged hard, broke
to the air, to the wind turning us scaly
with water?

The sleet blistered the pond, the ice groaned.
Then the first kick. And the hacking, the neighing,
till the roar we made broke up the dark
in the throats of dogs, the cattle bedded
in the field, broke by inches the black shell
of water, till the night
cracked like an egg shattered in the storm
of two beasts becoming one,
or one beast being born.

White Shrouds

From our kitchen window I watched the hard sleet chipping
at the granite pond, the white ducks
huddling in their giant mushroom, and felt against
my leg the warmth in the heater vent die.

Did you feel how cold it dropped that night?

At nine below, water expands into rock, the pipes peel
back like ripe fruit,
the heavy branches of the post oak bang like axes
against the house. The power fails
all over the neighborhood,
the ferns on the windowsill crack like china.

I went down to the basement to check the firewood,
wormy, maybe enough for one night,
then pulled the couch in front of a fireplace
too shallow for any real heat, wrapped you in a skin
of quilts, let you tuck and sleep
inside what comfort it gave.
On the end of the couch,
outside the eye and breath of the fire, ice
actually crusted the tips of my beard.
And in that other place where the cold takes you
out of yourself with each white breath,
I listened all night to the fanatical ministry
of the brain, the alarm
it sounds to keep the body alert,

which wasn't the ringing of bells over city shelters,
or the sirens of ambulances spinning out of alleys,

but was only that breathing,
the white easy breathing of sleepers curling
in doorways, behind dumpsters, their ears
slowly turning into stone, and no one
to husband the small logs, two at a time, onto the fire.

Ice

No one this far south chances ice.
So what was I to think when I sat down for breakfast
on the morning after Christmas
and saw through our glazed kitchen window
the whole pond frozen white,
and out of the stiff green pines on the far side
of the pond, our neighbor's teenage daughter
edging down the bank
one careful step at a time, a boot on a rock,
a boot on a ledge? She stopped at the lip of the ice,
picked up a rock large as a brick
and threw it out, watched it chip the surface
and slide. Then holding to a pine branch,
put one foot out and tried her weight.
I ran slow as a glacier,
or seemed to, as I pushed from the table,
and when she let go and shuffled away
from the bank, what could I do
but stand on my deck and shout the warning
that froze in the breath between us?
In the middle of the pond, all around her water
turned into something strange,
she began, of all things,
to shift on one leg, then the other,
each step sure as a prophecy,
each foot kicking thunder into the heads
of fish. Then up on her toes,
one leg sweeping her into a spin, arms flung out,
mittens like a blue dream circling her head.
And when she heard me and spun to a dizzy stop,
saw me in my ragged underwear,

barefoot on my deck,
when her hands came down to lift the hem
of an imaginary skirt
and she curtsied and turned and walked away,
I remembered a story her father told of growing up
poor in small-town Ohio,
how every year in the hard of winter
the mayor drove a rattletrap onto the river
and the lottery began.

Purple necks and green, fat drakes whiter than Easter
live on our five acres of suburban water
with one gray goose, a Canadian honker
who came a year ago and settled.
And occasionally other birds, locally exotic,
drop by the lake, a few gulls, an egret,
and once a wood ibis, all the thrill
of the neighborhood kids
coaxing them to stay with bread crumbs.
We know why these birds come to us, little stops
on ancient journeys, but the strangest of all
came straight from the blue, parcel post,
a prank gift or a mistake. One evening
we came home and found the box on the porch,
no return address. Inside was a plastic night-lamp,
orange bill, red body, pink feet,
gaudy, out of place anywhere in the house.

I unscrewed a bulb from a table lamp,
screwed it into the grassy base, plugged the cord
into an outlet, and cut the overhead.
Then in our living room something
out of science fiction! And possessed
we stared till that light sank in
and showed us the brilliance
of the one thing we were determined to do.

We pulled the extension cords from the typewriter
and the television, from the electric fan
cornered on the side porch,
took from the basement the fifty-foot cord

uncoupled from the weed-eater, dragged them all
into the backyard, where the sky leaned
black and defiant, strung them end on end
from the rear deck socket all the way to the edge
of the lake, propped the lamp
in the tall grass by the shallows.
On that water it burned like a returning god!
Not long then before the great goose, being
called, honked out into the cove,
the ducks breaking huddle on the bank,
dogs barking awake behind their fences,
until one by one in the houses around the lake
the upstairs windows lit up like eyes.

That goose still honks on the lake, all night,
haunted. And in the stories
of the neighborhood kids,
the ibis is commonplace, the snowy egret nothing
to speak of. There is only that sighting
too beautiful to believe, quick
and radiant as revelation,
and all their stories tell of a night
when lightning waddled down to the edge of the lake
to burn for a moment in the shape of a swan.

The Voice of Wives Dreaming

Some nights I wake to the cry of the child
who drowned in our pond,
and I crawl from my bed, dress,
leave my wife in her drift of sleep,
walk into the yard, down to the bank
where the water holds as many stars
as the sky. And if I ponder drifting out
onto that black heaven, if my arms
quiver like wings, I only stand
by the lip of the water and listen
for the voice disappearing,
the voice disappeared, the water.
And if the brush rattles I'm not startled.
I say, *Yes, it's happening again,*
and the vines crawling the oak limbs
rustle like a curtain as my neighbor walks
into the moon, points toward the far bank,
the thicket of pines, the flashlights
of other neighbors divining water.
We meet them again by the earth dam
and give the hard testimony,
who first saw the body blooming white
as a lily in the oak roots,
who untangled the grassy drifts of hair,
who pried the fingers from the ball
of the sun. And repeat our stories
of other mornings, the eyes of our women
startled out of sleep, their hands still
shaky at the table, spilling coffee,
the frightful talk. So long ago now
you'd think we might lose a thing

like a flower under the knee of an oak,
but in the women the current moves
another way. Or so we account for it
as we back into the woods, onto
the trails along the bank, knowing
in this we account for nothing,
can only gather, listen, witness,
then stagger off, wakeful,
toward our own backyards, the deck lights
edging the doorways we enter
to find again that communal drift of sleep
where each woman floats face down
dreaming the voice of a different child.

The Guitar

Alone on a hill above the festival, I listen past field noise
to the single bird note humming
off the prongs of a metal fork, and twist the keys
of my guitar, flat, then sharper, trying to pull
all loose tension into line, to rest each bronze string
on the one clean level of sound all musicians strive for.

Then across the hill walks a fiddler coming from another jam,
his bow pointing me out in the dark, his fiddle
fluttering under his chin, "Bill Cheatum"
already bridging the distance between us.

How long before his ear, pitched to those bright true notes,
brings to his face the blank disappointment of the moon,
and he saws the tune short,
walks off toward the field, the notes rising like sparks
around the campfires?

And these nights when you come home late from work
or whatever, highstrung
and restless, and already turned in
I'm a case of insomnia, each sorry fret buzzing in my head,
or if by chance asleep, awakened
by your little torches of sound, the low opera
of a late-night movie, the click of your lighter—

how long do I lie in that room, waiting for a footfall,
the bright run of bracelets,
wondering how a night could be as wide as a field,
and why, when you lie down beside me, both of us silent,
I wonder again at the guitar, how anything studied so long
could suddenly go strange in my hand?

In Heritage Farms, Settled

In their tennis whites, their pastel Izods, all day the women
walk down my street, their Coppertoned children
sleek as seals, trailing to the courts
and the pool.

Through my wall of loose screen I watch the neighborhood,
the mowers, the gardeners, the crew
of movers wrestling with a van of Early American.

What worries me most is this constant settling,
my dog refusing to bark at joggers, content to stalk
to the edge of the porch, whimper back
to his nap, his muscular breathing.

Sometimes for no reason, gravity seems to surge,
the house trembles and the foundation sinks
a little deeper into the lawn.
Then the Volvos crawl through the street, and neighbors
read a month of mail beside their boxes, water
the same pink rose for hours.

This is when I force myself into the yard,
when I blow through the woods bordering the pond,
kicking colonies of mushrooms, the stinkhorns,
the devil's urns, when I make tracks and look for tracks,
following the creek with its cargo
of debris, desperate for something to praise,

something small and changing,
the delicate white maggot wagging in its cradle
of turds, the tiny feet of the tadpole, every leg
of the hornworm inching toward the wings of the phoenix moth.

Arcana Mundi

Once again the heavens cast their cosmical hocus-pocus
over the oily parking lot
of Tito's Italian Restaurant.

Inside Blind Willie's,
Joel "The Blues Prophet" Murphy tunes his Telecaster
to the harp of Chicago Bob. The room quietens.

Sometimes after the crowds have gone,
and the waitresses and the bartender have given up
on busing the room, out on this freight dock,

with the lights from Tito's off and the Texaco station
across the street black as the final embargo,
sometimes, then, over a last drink

of Gordon's, I get so entranced by the stars swelling
in the black sky, I believe they're busting
to tell me something.

Over the flat roof of the Majik Mart, the moon slowly
levitates, and practices her psychokinesis
all over Virginia Highlands.

I'm weak. I follow her across the roof, the spire
of Soul Harbor. And sometimes she seems so fat
with answers, I follow her

all the way into the trees along Highland, hopped up
on the gin, the blues, believing
the great *Arcana Mundi* might actually be revealed.

But what's revealed is only the ancient history of fate,
where someone on the edge of something
goes out of his head. Like this freight dock

when the moon drops again behind her darkest veil
and the neighborhood goes yuppie and safe,
and the most I can divine

is that I'm alone again
above the gray and empty parking lot of Tito's Italian,
watching the stars shrink in the black sky.

I'd dared her to go in, and we came on that dare
to the road above Rose Hill Cemetery,
and sat for a moment in the cab of my truck,
quiet, not talking, looking down
at the valley of stones, the bone-white
testaments prickling the hills.
All the way out she talked of death, her desire
to be cremated, have her ashes scattered
over Lake Rabun. In the new life she'd return
as a swan or a dove. What did I say?
That I believed in the new life too,
the resurrection of the body, and though I knew
the Lord could mend us ash by ash
I wasn't the sort to put Him to the trouble.
So I wasn't afraid, we were as different
as East and West, and the night was still cool,
not quite the season to fall in love
with the wrong woman. And if she was afraid
of anything, she didn't show it, only took
the flashlight off the seat, zipped her parka.
A bright half-moon, white as marble, hung
over the river, and I followed her
in that light as she edged through the trees
down the hill toward the gardens,
toward the creek, the row of bricked vaults.
I'd dared her to go in. Not into the graveyard,
but into a grave I knew lay open in the side
of a ridge, an old haunt, reputed hangout
of a witches' coven. And I wasn't afraid
until I stopped where the rock garden
bridges the creek, and the wind off the river

seemed the breath of the dead, or whatever
inside me was dying. *Let's go,* she said,
and pointed up the ridge where I had pointed
to the grave, and we followed the creek
up the valley, past the wrought-iron fences
and chairs, the patios and bedrooms
of the dead, without talking, without touching
or ever having touched, until we came
to the end of the valley, the black mouth
gaping behind branches. She knelt then
by the tree and shined the light—
wine bottles, a sardine can, stubs of iron bars
jagging those jaws with rusty teeth—
and with only a slight shiver against the cold,
we crawled into that belly of earth.
And what had I really expected to find? A pit
of beer cans, a clay chamber of dry roots?
Or that stir in the sudden falling of dark,
like the brush of a cobweb against an ear,
like the silky crawl of the first hungry worm,
the gentlest touch,
that first delicate laying on of hands?

II

An Old Hymn for Ian Jenkins

All things we value in terms of contrast,
the Ian Jenkins walking tour of New York
taught me that. Chelsea, the Bowery,
Little Italy, the long track
across Chinatown, my round eyes opening
to the light of the immigrant East.
And in the Garden of the Golden Dragon,
you dissecting my displacement,
punctuating with the click of chopsticks
the Jenkins theory of urban alienation.
That analogy of the hive-dweller,
his drone-like problems with identity,
that whole argument for territory,
sinks in now with the sunlight raining
through the gaps in these trees.
And as we cross the field from the house
to the pond, still groggy from the Mets
game, the late miles on the turnpike,
I know why you and the Upper West Side
zip to these mountains on weekends.
Last night, through the dead black
of time, a horse snorted in the woods,
a carriage rocked down the wheel ruts
of the road and stopped in front
of the house. Downstairs the front door
slapped closed, and cards fluttered
like wings across tables, all I remember
of the house showing my sleep the past.
And what it neglected of the grounds,
the field where the local militia drilled
for the Revolution, the Colonial graveyard

at the foot of the hill, you fill in,
from landmark to landmark, piecing time
and dirt like the rags of history's quilt.
I understand that. Southerners know
how a place can wrap you up in a dream.
And what this place puts me in mind of,
the clear river edging the green field,
the solid house beyond the graves,
are the elements of an old hymn,
Flatt and Scruggs wide open on your stereo,
their mansion over the hilltop, their land
of beautiful flowers where we'll never
grow old. What I'm talking about
is that place we go to save ourselves,
that place in the dream where the object
of the dream is place.

Gospel Banjo: Homage to Little Roy Lewis

Three days I lay with a fire under my skin, in the guest room,
in the twin bed by the window.

The preacher in waist-high water, his Bible, the walnut frame,
the footboard, everything
shimmied in heat, the lights mostly down,
the brightest thing in the room
the banjo cracking in the speakers of the stereo.

That last night I fell into a dream of a river, a cold wind
brushing my arms straight out
toward the gray water, open and deep, too wide to see across.
And anchored on that bank, a little white boat
wormy with scars.

Little Roy, can you imagine that long drift,
the tenuous ark of the dream
like a single note sailing farther and farther from the string?

All I remember is waking under the full moon floating
in the window,
the shell of your Mastertone swimming in a tablature of stars.

Little Roy, to come back to anything as clear and bright
as your banjo, to watch the stars
wink off every note,

to roll toward the room and hear each riff spark
across the distance,
and to ease back, cool and clear-headed,
alive and listening,
is to hear the dream flaunting the possibility of the dream,
which is the joy of waking on either side of the Jordan.

Homage to Lester Flatt

Troublesome waters I'm fearing no more

Five seasons without traveling to a festival, without walking
into a field and hearing that voice.

And now after a long spell of rain, I step off my porch
and walk toward the river,
remembering the last time I saw Lester Flatt,
how thin he looked and sick
as he sat back in a lawn chair under the sagging pines
of Lavonia, Georgia,
and scribbled his name on the jackets of records.

How do the roots chord, Lester?
And the click beetle and the cricket, the cicada, the toad,
what harmonies do they sing in the high grass?

All of those voices
want me to praise your remarkable voice—

Tonight little sparks are winking in the fields, and the dead
are combing the edge of the forest, their arms
full of campfires.
Tonight the dead are building a stage under a funeral tent
and blowing the dust off banjos.
Tonight, for you, the dead are shaking the worms
from their ears.

Lester, singing whatever we want to about the dead
is the easiest thing in the world.
Believing it the hardest.
So this is where I stop, in this wet grass.
This is the river we're all troubled by, where the storm wash
rattling the bank echoes the tenor of our lives.

Face Jugs: Homage to Lanier Meaders

From the tailgate of a pickup on the shoulder of Georgia 52,
from the crafts tent at the White County Fair,
the right face may find you,

or from the wall of the mountain store at Tallulah Gorge,
one face shelved among his many brothers,
the pig-face, the devil-face, the moon-face, may turn
just the right way in the light
in the leaves, in the light tinted by gingham, by walls
of doll clothes and pastel quilts, may turn
to you, his eyes stunned awake by the knowledge
that yours is the face he was meant for.

There is nothing to do then but lift him from the shelf,
nothing to do but hold him
by the window where the light from the wavy pane
makes a mirror of his glaze, your eyes
swimming in his gouged sockets, your cleft on his chin,
your lips floating over his tongue.

You hear again what that tongue is fired to say, the old
admonishment, the clay and the flesh.
But he is simply you, and as you walk to the car,
happy as a man who's found his puzzle's missing piece,
it frightens you to think you might have left him.

And when you get home to the city,
when you move the crystal cherub into the dining room
and place the fern on the mantle, when you
polish the end table and ease him down on slick mahogany,
all you feel is gratitude. And you relax on the sofa,
smiling at the melon head, the pancake cheeks,
the yellow, rock-toothed mouth grinning back in deep relief.

III

Awake

A winter so hard you think the shrubs may never rouse,
the redtips stunned in their brown coma,
the boxwoods flaking like pillows of rust.
Then one day, weeks late,
the first bud winks on the China tree,
and the maple sapling, leafless,
sends a green tentative feeler
into the yard. Underground
something is stirring, climbing through the veins.

That night the shadows leave a warmth in the air,
a promising stillness,
so you take your rod and tackle box,
you walk the quarter mile of thickening woods,
stand in the weedy mire bordering the shallows,
ease your fly onto the surface.

And you see in what light the stars give the lake
a wavy V zagging the water, a spade head
running the brush shadows, vanishing,
and the water smoothing to a plate of black glass.
The wind blows the honeysuckle
out of the pines, and the surface ripples easy
with the drift of twigs and feathers.
The old needles alert the new leaves,
the fly jitters under a bush.
A gray breath of fog yawns out of the cove
and the tail washes up on your boot.

Gar

All night the river house swayed
on stilts, and mosquitos navigated the slit screen to find me
asleep on the top bunk and salty with sweat.
From a dream of fish
their kisses stung me into the stifling heat
and the steam rising off the river,
and I rose dazed and found my clothes,
my line and my tackle.

A red sun bobbed into the rushes
and pricked the skin of the river, long needles of blood
stabbing the bank where a ribbon snake slipped
off a root and into the water, where a skink climbed
a brown stone, where my reel whined
at the river thrashing under the rush shadows, a rusty snout,
a saw blade from the old world, hacking
like a memory at the light.

Rats at Allatoona

Over the lake the stars scatter their crumbs of light,
shadows skirt the pines, the docks
treading the cove,
and through those shadows rats ease toward the campsites,
the metal drums rich with the garbage
of weekenders.
                    I listen, drunk, on this deck
as their feet fill up the dark. Above the crickets
and the soft lap of water,
they pray a squeaky grace of fine nails climbing
the rusty sides of cans.
                              Tonight I'm dreaming
of walking out toward them, of stumbling over the rocks
toward the cove, blind as a shadow, homing
on their rapture. I'm dreaming of lying down
beside them and feeling on my neck in the boozy wave
of sleep the first whisker, a moist
nose, the needle comb of a paw,
and of stirring in sunlight in the wet grass
of the cove, among cans
and ashes, shreds of their sacrament, of fingering
my hair and my face, waking
to what I am in my dream and my body, whole
and broken, having taken from the feast
and given to it, the tip of a thumb, the lobe of an ear.

The Offering

Into the scrap pine I jerked the saw blade, guessing dimensions,
leaving the edges rough. And the boards I cut
I tacked into a crude feeder,
two simple shelves like open hands.

I took my ladder to the corner of the yard where a willow
hangs over the pond, and poured into the feeder
the mixed seeds of five grasses,
hung those shelves in the top of that tree.

Days passed before any birds trusted enough to come,
then together came the blackbirds and the sparrows.

And for hours on my porch
I gave myself to the catbirds, the mockingbirds
who held in their throats the voices
of all the neighborhood beasts, known and unknown.

But eventually not even their songs were enough,
where was the voice they couldn't mimic?

Now at night I wait on my porch, anxious
with my tiny guilt.
And I rock back in my chair, watch with my night glasses
the dark jaw of pinetops,
the trees on the edge of the pond, the willow trembling
under the feeder where the dead mouse lies in the starlight,
fat as a tongue, white as a soul.

Under the Vulture-Tree

We have all seen them circling pastures,
have looked up from the mouth of a barn, a pine clearing,
the fences of our own backyards, and have stood
amazed by the one slow wing beat, the endless dihedral drift.
But I had never seen so many so close, hundreds,
every limb of the dead oak feathered black,

and I cut the engine, let the river grab the jon boat
and pull it toward the tree.
The black leaves shined, the pink fruit blossomed
red, ugly as a human heart.
Then, as I passed under their dream, I saw for the first time
its soft countenance, the raw fleshy jowls
wrinkled and generous, like the faces of the very old
who have grown to empathize with everything.

And I drifted away from them, slow, on the pull of the river,
reluctant, looking back at their roost,
calling them what I'd never called them, what they are,
those dwarfed transfiguring angels,
who flock to the side of the poisoned fox, the mud turtle
crushed on the shoulder of the road,
who pray over the leaf-graves of the anonymous lost,
with mercy enough to consume us all and give us wings.

On the Willow Branch

Now the pond is still and the softest paddle stroke eases
the boat into the cove. Over the floating stars
you drift, the water settles around you.

The eyes widen as the body remembers,
the stars flare over the pines.
Down cove the tree frogs line their favorite hymns
and the wood drake listens.
At your fingertips the water strider performs
his nightly miracle.

Then a branch above the jon boat rustles like breath
and you look up. Nothing,
then the rustle again, and you shine the light.

Red eyes spark on the willow leaves,
flare, selfless,
and suddenly you're ashamed of your loneliness.

The wind gusts hard on the pond, and the branch sways
out of your beam. The jon boat tosses
easy in the wave-slap, and the old brain clings
to the spine.

IV

Fiddle Time

Off the fiddle of a man who rented a garage from my father
came the first music
I remember hearing. His name is lost and his face,
but I remember the sparrows nesting
in his rafters, and the boxes of shatterproof auto glass,
the rolls of vinyl and cloth, the heavy Singer
for stitching seat covers.
And how seldom he did
any upholstery business or worried about that business
as he leaned over his plywood bench
in sunlight edging through gaps where sheets of red tin
hung loose or rusted away from the roof,
sanding for hours the swell of a close-grained face,
the taper of a neck, an f-hole.

And I remember clearly those Sunday afternoons, his bow
sparking rosin off the fiddle strings,
the strained face of the guitar player, a beat behind,
a beat ahead, though I can't recall one tune they played,
not a snatch of a melody.
The truth is
he wasn't that smooth a fiddler. But he cared
for the fiddle, and in the memory's raw first music
I still catch a measure of that care,
a jigsaw blade, a gruff file humming,
or the sandpaper rasping in the tips of his fingers
as he shuffles time,
not quite lost, over the curve of a finely honed bridge.

A Tent Beside a River

Remembering lanterned, canvas-sprawled fields
of the county, we gathered for dream's sake
under the roof of the blue nylon tent,
opened Bible and Baptist hymnal
under a flashlight's yellow stain
to call into play our own miracle. And afraid
we'd be found out of bed, sang in whispers
the few songs we could sing, to be heard
only by the One we wanted to hear.
Then I, who could read best, read what
I could from the Scripture, my breath
the rustle of leaves over a lip of open water.
For in the house at the yard's heart,
our grandfather lay dreaming of Jordan,
his face gone pale as the light shining
through his curtained window, a lamp
they would not turn off, as though it kept
him from crossing by anchoring his shadow
beside him. For an hour in the yard
choirs of crickets echoed hymns
and short winds chorded the trees.
Then far off in the tall dark of pines
beyond the house, an owl with a voice deeper
than time announced the lateness of the hour.
We were new at grief, and weak,
and let ourselves fall toward sleep,
forgot the house and the lamp, the old man
wrestling his shadow. But this is not
entirely true. When the tent flap snared
the dark, a light came on behind our eyes,
and each of us saw him a special way.

Then the owl came down to find us, whistled
a note of departure, and we remembered,
real or not, a shadow drifting over the roof.
They found us, too, in morning light, huddled
in a ball like a litter of strays,
and rousted us with voices nervy and crisp
as the air, as though children
had never dreamed of such,
nor their words ferried anyone safely anywhere.

A Model Shelter

Single file in our blue uniforms, saluting with two fingers
the public on Main Street,
we marched behind Mrs. Jones, mother of Den 6.

The first leaves had littered the sidewalk, and a convict
raked them into piles on the courthouse lawn.
We edged past that lesson in civics, up the marble steps
and onto the portico,
where Mrs. Jones stopped us under the eagles and counted heads.
No one lost to the Saturday traffic,
to Kessler's 5 & 10, the fountain at Canton Pharmacy,
we wound into the lobby, down the stairway
into the basement, past the office of the County Clerk,
into a room marked *Shelter*.

Like the caverns of Carlsbad, the caves at Rock City,
it was enough to give you the shivers.
Everyone touched a concrete wall,
no one giggled at the naked toilet.

Mrs. Jones stood us in the center of the room,
opened the medicine chest, the kit for decontamination.
She cranked a handle in one wall
and cold air whirred through a vent in the ceiling.
Bottled water, blankets, extra clothing, and enough food,
she said, to hold two families all winter.
I thought of the black bears in the *Boy's Life*
she kept on the table by her sofa.

How long could they live curled around themselves?
And the children in Russia, the little cubs of the Soviet,
into what damp caves were they crawling?

Shingling the New Roof

On the roof of the garage my father was hammering into a house
I tacked on shingles with the men,
carried nails up and down the ladder, and made a wage.

Four of us up there among the limbs that kept the sun
off one whole side of the house,
our neighbor, my father, and my grandfather
whose house it was to become. Four of us finishing the roof,

and my mother sending up Cokes and sandwiches
in a bucket strung over a limb. My mother telling me to watch
my step, to stay away from the ledge, telling my father
I was too small to be on the roof.
                                        And maybe I was,
but I didn't think so, even when I jerked too hard
on a stubborn nail and tumbled, hammer-loose,
into a backward somersault, feet upside down into the air
above the yard, hands just hooking the gutter.

I remember my body dangling fifteen feet above the spikes
of the picket fence,
and my father's face, whiter than caulk, as he scrambled
toward the ledge, his steel fist and arm hoisting me, one tug,
to the solid roof.

On the back porch my mother stood absolutely silent, a dishrag
twisted in her hands, and I remember the expression
that passed from her face to his.
                                        What did I do?
The rest of that day I sat on the porch
where I watched them moving easily in the limbs of the oak
and felt on my wrist under the face of my watch
a sharp impression deepening to a bruise.

Under a sky of stars and no moon, in the curve of headlights
alarming the county,
a line of deputies wades through a field
of waist-high hay. By a wall of gray pine at the edge
of that field, something curls, glows
bright as blood.
                                        I curl under my blanket,
watch the yellow dial on the radio, the stars hanging
in the black panes of the window. This is real,
not make-believe horror, metallic, alive,
ultimately alien,

and the deputies trailing paths in the hay
move toward it, inch by inch, as the voice of the reporter
rises bodiless in my room, wind in his microphone
like a siren whistling the end of the world
as we know it. And I remember, vaguely, a night
my father carried me into,
a sky of loud crickets, a field of stars, a radio tower,
and circling the red light of that tower, two unknown lights,
balls of blue and green.

What those deputies find at the end of that field,
a piece of broken sign,
the letter O in fluorescent red, is nothing to ease my sleep.
I dream of the whole universe, of an infinite
and indiscriminate creation
where the black frontier behind the eyes floats back as far
as the light behind the stars.

Wings

What was it she taught
that the whole room had to be haunted by birds?

That night the telephone rang,
A crow on the mountain needs her wings clipped.
Why wasn't a question they thought to ask
when they gathered, four of them,
in the layered dark under the pine branches
on the hill overlooking the colored school.

The first one down kicked the latch, and the door
swung back. They closed it behind them
and felt through the room, wedging
into chairs, catching the moonlight that fell
through the windows. Which wasn't much,
but enough to see a buzzard
spreading black wings over a bookcase.
What in the world, somebody said,
then stood up and struck a match. A red bird
glared from a wall perch, then a jay,
a martin, a robin. A sparrow hawk
climbed the wall, talons balled on dusty fur.
When the match went out, a story
went around of a gypsy who could change herself
into a hawk. All across the county, not a hen
was safe. *I never heard such nonsense,*
someone said. Someone else struck a match
and held it in his face,
It's only a story, and shook it out.

Light rose like red smoke over the hill of pines
and flooded the window,
threw them all under the shadow of wings.

From the back of the room, a barn owl gazed
across a kingdom of birds, the mourning dove
flushed into the field of light,
the quail, the sparrow, the mockingbird,
all flying on strings under the blue ceiling.
Birds, somebody said, and pointed a finger
like a gun. *Hush,*
outside, down the hill,
an engine, cylinders knocking like a bad heart.

They held their noise as the engine choked,
a door squeaked shut, light feet crossed cinders.
She stopped for a second on the stoop
while the broken latch rattled
on its hinge. Then wind swung the door, and all
through the schoolhouse
birds spooked under the wooden sky.

Good morning, she said, cool as the wind,
which didn't sit well with any of them.
In the wide-open door she stood, frail,
thin as a twig, and stared at the top of her desk.
Come to chop us some wood?

What was it she taught
in her school that a man could be haunted by wings,
could see one crow on a fence,
a grackle, the shadow
of a hawk, and find his hand flying up to his eyes?

What charms did she study
that in their memory a hand hacked loose from a wrist
could flap across a desk and fly away?

The Window

On Allgood Road two miles off Georgia 41, you round a curve
canopied by pine
and the house leaps out of the trees to meet you.

Upstairs in the far right window she waited for us,
she rocked in the shadows
of the wide magnolia. After school, newly licensed
by the state, we came to her in pairs, in carloads
leaning into that curve, reckless
on spirits, our hearts thrown to her
by the physics of desire,
and swore, no matter what speed we tore from the wheels
of our fathers, we'd seen her
in the upstairs window, a blossom of magnolia
in her hair.
These affairs got quickly out of hand,
other boys from other schools following suit,
and soon signs were posted,
the shade pulled down on that room for good.
But we came anyway, at night, in caravans
to see her silhouette in the window, evidence enough.

How long did this go on? All spring and summer,
until one boy threw caution too far into that curve.
After that they sealed the window with mortar and brick,
the room itself the shadow of a crypt.

That was half my life ago, and I've not swerved since
into the wrong lane of any curve. Nor forgotten
that house, the thick wreath
of magnolia branches, the zodiac
of white blossoms surrounding the window, the presence
waiting in that room, patient and promiscuous.

In Louisiana

Fog solid on the pond, I went anyway on that first cool night
of fall, staggering downhill
through wet grass, arms full of tackle, a boat motor,
toward the fence to be climbed and the jon boat
stuck on the mud beach,
and made it over that fence and halfway to the water
before the one root I stumbled over flew up and struck me
just below the knee.

For a long time I saw nothing
in dreams, then there was my father wading in the swamp, fog
like breath around his waist, and his arms
reaching into that fog, into the water
it hovered over somewhere in Louisiana, among roots
and other things hidden,
bringing up in his hands a tail like a copperhead's
but arm-thick and long,
as he dragged up thrashing on the other end
no head of a snake, but the chest and head of a boy,
his fingers still tangled in a knot of roots.
Always I'll remember
that gaped mouth drooling sludge, those dull fish eyes
wide in the new light
like the stunned eyes of the dying.
And that boy's face
changing around them into all the faces
I've seen enter that border of fog, struggling, beyond
help, as they stare fish-blind into the light of hospitals,
into the sun darkening the lips of ditches
and soggy fields,
their dumb, stunned eyes already clouding,
looking for one root,
the corner of a bed sheet, anything in the world to clutch.

V

Naval Photograph: 25 October 1942: What the Hand May Be Saying

Reports of a Japanese surface presence have brought them
   speeding
into Savo Sound,
false reports that will not be true for days.

So now at evening the fleet drops anchor, the crews relax,
the heat drifts west toward the war in Africa.

On the deck of the tender *Tangier*
a sailor focuses a camera on a foreground of water,
the cruiser *Atlanta,* and far back against the jungles of Savo
the hulks of Task Group 66.4.

A few on the cruiser notice him, but you cannot tell it
from their faces, too many shadows, too long a stretch
of grainy water. Still,
figures can be seen loafing on the bow, leaning
from the bridge, the machine gun platforms, even a sailor
clowning on a gun turret, barrel straight up between his legs.

And behind the shadow draped like armor across that stern,
my father is standing with the gunners
under turret number six, a shadow
in a wide cluster of shadows waving toward the *Tangier.*

Knowing their future, I imagine
some pulse in the nerves, primitive as radar, throbbing,

and exactly what the hand is saying, even he does not know.
He is only standing where the living and the dead
lean against the rail,
unsure who is who, and wave across the sound
toward the camera, toward us, for all of the reasons anyone waves.

The Anniversary

This is the night I come to my room,
a bottle of brandy, or whiskey, a glass,
and close the door on the rest of the house,
pull the shades, switch off the lights,
imagine a darkness just as it may have been.
I pull my chair to the middle of the room,
fall to it like a man with a mission,
and do not turn on the radio, the stereo,
as I might do on any other night,
but listen to the pines brush the house
with a sound like the bow of a ship
rising and falling through water.
Then I drink for the shakes and I get them
when I see again jarring the darkness
the terrible rising sun, the searchlight
of the *Hiei* stabbing across the sound,
and jolt in my chair as the turret slues,
guns already deafening the long light blind.
Look, there he is at the door of the turret
and then, God, the blast of the shell
kicks him right back out! Then, God . . .
what? For this is the night my father,
forehead shattered, side pierced, was thrown
for dead from the deck of the *Atlanta*,
toward a place that was not Guadalcanal
or Florida Island, drifted like a man dead
to the world ending around him, and was dead
to the arms of the sailors in the lifeboat,
dead as any drunk in any armchair
who trembles at the horror of his thoughts
and learns, as he learns every year,

that the power in the blood to terrify
is sometimes the power of love. So moves
one knee trembling toward his desk,
stands on shaky legs and puts down his glass,
leans on the desk and opens the drawer,
feels for the small pearl-handled knife,
the sharpest blade of Japanese steel,
This is your blood in remembrance of you,
who died one night at sea and lived,
brings it to his face, brings it to his eye,
touches with the nervous point
the flesh of his forehead, an old scar.

The Desk

Under the fire escape, crouched, one knee in cinders,
I pulled the ball-peen hammer from my belt,
cracked a square of window pane,
the gummed latch, and swung the window,
crawled through that stone hole into the boiler room
of Canton Elementary School, once Canton High,
where my father served three extra years
as star halfback and sprinter.
Behind a flashlight's
cane of light, I climbed a staircase almost a ladder
and found a door. On the second nudge of my shoulder,
it broke into a hallway dark as history,
at whose end lay the classroom I had studied
over and over in the deep obsession of memory.

I swept that room with my light—an empty blackboard,
a metal table, a half-globe lying on the floor
like a punctured basketball—then followed
that beam across the rows of desks,
the various catalogs of lovers, the lists
of all those who would and would not do what,
until it stopped on the corner desk of the back row,
and I saw again, after many years, the name
of my father, my name, carved deep into the oak top.

To gauge the depth I ran my finger across that scar,
and wondered at the dreams he must have lived
as his eyes ran back and forth
from the cinder yard below the window
to the empty practice field
to the blade of his pocket knife etching carefully

the long, angular lines of his name,
the dreams he must have laid out one behind another
like yard lines, in the dull, pre-practice afternoons
of geography and civics, before he ever dreamed
of Savo Sound or Guadalcanal.

In honor of dreams
I sank to my knees on the smooth, oiled floor,
and stood my flashlight on its end.
Half the yellow circle lit the underedge of the desk,
the other threw a half-moon on the ceiling,
and in that split light I tapped the hammer
easy up the overhang of the desk top. Nothing gave
but the walls' sharp echo, so I swung again,
and again harder, and harder still in half anger
rising to anger at the stubborn joint, losing all fear
of my first crime against the city, the county,
the state, whatever government claimed dominion,
until I had hammered up in the ringing dark
a salvo of crossfire, and on a frantic recoil glanced
the flashlight, the classroom spinning black
as a coma.

I've often pictured the face of the teacher
whose student first pointed to that topless desk,
the shock of a slow hand rising from the back row,
their eyes meeting over the question of absence.
I've wondered too if some low authority of the system
discovered that shattered window,
and finding no typewriters, no business machines,
no audiovisual gear missing, failed to account for it,
so let it pass as minor vandalism.

I've heard nothing.
And rarely do I fret when I see that oak scar leaning
against my basement wall, though I wonder what it means
to own my father's name.

NOTES

"Ice" is for Dave Smith, "Awake" for Barry Hannah, "Fiddle Time" for Kelly Jean Beard, and "Under the Vulture-Tree" for Mary Oliver.

"Gospel Banjo: Homage to Little Roy Lewis" is inspired by the music of The Lewis Family of Lincolnton, Georgia.

"Face Jugs: Homage to Lanier Meaders" is inspired by the pottery of the Meaders family of White County, Georgia.

David Bottoms was born in Canton, Georgia, in 1949. His poems have appeared widely in such magazines as *Atlantic Monthly, The New Yorker, Harper's, Poetry,* and *American Poetry Review,* as well as in numerous anthologies. His first book, *Shooting Rats at the Bibb County Dump,* was chosen by Robert Penn Warren as winner of the 1979 Walt Whitman Award of the Academy of American Poets; his second book, *In a U-Haul North of Damascus,* was named Book of the Year in Poetry by the Dixie Council of Authors and Journalists; and a group of poems from *Under the Vulture-Tree* was awarded the Levinson Prize from *Poetry* magazine. He is also the author of a novel, *Any Cold Jordan,* and is co-editor (with Dave Smith) of *The Morrow Anthology of Younger American Poets.* He lives in Atlanta, where he teaches creative writing at Georgia State University.